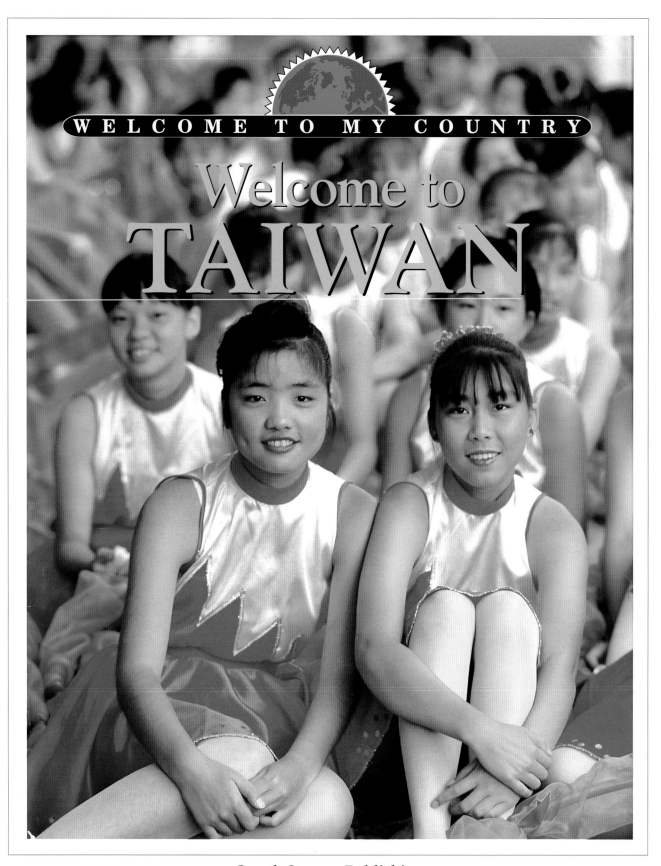

WELCOME TO MY COUNTRY

Welcome to
TAIWAN

Gareth Stevens Publishing
A WORLD ALMANAC EDUCATION GROUP COMPANY

Written by
VANESSA WAN

Edited by
MELVIN NEO

Edited in USA by
JENETTE DONOVAN GUNTLY

Designed by
GEOSLYN LIM

Picture research by
SUSAN JANE MANUEL

First published in North America in 2005 by
Gareth Stevens Publishing
A World Almanac Education Group Company
330 West Olive Street, Suite 100
Milwaukee, Wisconsin 53212 USA

Please visit our web site at
www.garethstevens.com
For a free color catalog describing
Gareth Stevens Publishing's list of high-quality
books and multimedia programs,
call 1-800-542-2595 (USA) or
1-800-387-3178 (Canada).
Gareth Stevens Publishing's fax: (414) 332-3567.

© **MARSHALL CAVENDISH INTERNATIONAL (ASIA)**
PRIVATE LIMITED 2004
Originated and designed by
Times Editions Marshall Cavendish
An imprint of Marshall Cavendish International (Asia) Pte Ltd
A member of Times Publishing Limited
Times Centre, 1 New Industrial Road
Singapore 536196
http://www.timesone.com.sg/te

Library of Congress Cataloging-in-Publication Data
Wan, Vanessa.
Welcome to Taiwan / Vanessa Wan.
p. cm. — (Welcome to my country)
Includes bibliographical references and index.
ISBN 0-8368-3122-5 (lib. bdg.)
1. Taiwan — Juvenile literature. [1. Taiwan.] I. Title. II. Series.
DS799.W34   2004
951.24'9—dc22   2004046688

Printed in Singapore

1 2 3 4 5 6 7 8 9 08 07 06 05 04

PICTURE CREDITS
Art Directors and TRIP Photo Library:
  3 (bottom), 5, 6, 7, 8, 9 (top), 18, 27,
  32, 34, 35 (top), 38 (top), 39, 45
Bes Stock Photo Library: cover, 1, 24, 31
Michelle Burgess: 9 (bottom)
Focus Team — Italy: 4, 22, 43
Getty Images/Hulton Archive: 10, 12, 14,
  15 (top), 37
The Hutchison Library: 2, 3 (top and center),
  16, 17, 21 (top), 25, 29, 33, 40
Lonely Planet Images: 38 (bottom)
North Wind Picture Archives: 11
David Simson: 13, 19, 20, 21 (bottom),
  23, 26 (top), 28 (both), 30, 35 (bottom),
  36, 41 (both)
Taiwan Visitors Center: 15 (bottom)
Travel Ink Photo and Feature Library:
  26 (bottom)

Digital Scanning by Superskill Graphics Pte Ltd

Contents

Words that appear in the glossary are printed in **boldface** type the first time they occur in the text.

Welcome to Taiwan!

Taiwan is a group of islands located off the coast of **mainland** China. Although it is officially part of China, Taiwan has its own government. Taiwan is known for the **technology** it produces and for its busy, crowded cities, but it is also a country of beautiful mountains and many kinds of wildlife. Let's explore Taiwan and learn about its people!

Opposite: A crowd gathers to watch the changing of the guard at the Revolutionary **Martyrs'** Shrine in the city of Taipei.

Below: Children wave Taiwan's national flag as they celebrate Double Tenth National Day on October 10.

The Flag of Taiwan

Taiwan's flag was adopted on December 17, 1928. The blue, white, and red of the flag are symbols of loyalty to the nation, rule by the people, and social well-being. The points of the white star represent the twelve periods of two hours that make up a day.

The Land

Taiwan has an area of 13,888 square miles (35,980 square kilometers). It is made up of the main island, which is also called Taiwan, and the Penghu **Archipelago**. Taiwan is surrounded by the East China Sea, the Pacific Ocean, the Philippine Sea, the South China Sea, and the Taiwan Strait.

Left: Hot springs pool on the beaches of Lutao, or Green Island. Lutao is one of the islands of the Penghu Archipelago and is located off the east coast of the island of Taiwan.

Left: Yu Shan, or Mount Jade, is the highest point on the main island of Taiwan. It measures about 13,113 feet (3,997 meters) high.

Half of the main island of Taiwan is covered by a mountain range called the *Chungyang Shanmo* (CHONG-yuhng SHUHN-mor) mountains. They were formed by old volcanoes that are no longer active. Heat rising from the old volcanoes has formed hot springs on the high mountain ridges. The east side of the mountains end in steep cliffs that face the Pacific Ocean. To the west of the mountains are small hills and plains. The island also has over one hundred rivers and streams.

Climate

Southern Taiwan's climate is tropical, or very warm and damp. The northern mountain regions are cooler and dryer. Taiwan has a northern and a southern **monsoon** season. The monsoon season in the south often includes typhoons, which are big storms with very strong winds and heavy rain. The northern monsoon season usually includes heavy rainfall that can total up to 99 inches (2,515 millimeters) of rain each year.

Above: A skier looks out over the snowy slopes of Hohuan Shan. Snow is common on the high mountains of northern Taiwan.

Plants and Animals

Many different kinds of trees grow in Taiwan, including evergreen trees on the high mountains. Junipers, Japanese cedars, and rhododendrons grow in the hills and lower mountains. Palm trees grow in the low areas. Many animals live in Taiwan, including goats, deer, and wild boars. Formosan macaques, a type of monkey, live in the low-lying mountains of Taiwan. The country also has about five hundred different kinds of birds, including geese and pheasants.

Above: Poinsettias came from Mexico originally, but they grow well in parts of Taiwan, including around the banks of Sun Moon Lake.

Left:
The muntjac is also called the barking deer because of its call, which sounds like a barking dog. It is **native** to China and Taiwan.

History

The first people to live in what is now Taiwan were the Malayan-Polynesian people. Later, groups of Chinese people came to the island, causing the native people to move to the mountain areas.

People from the West first arrived in Taiwan in the 1500s. The Dutch arrived in the early 1620s. They settled in the southwest, where they built churches and forts and grew sugarcane and rice.

Left: A Dutch explorer named Jan Huyghen van Linschoten (1563–1611) was one of the first people from the West to visit Taiwan. He called the island "Ilha Formosa," which means "beautiful island." Taiwan was known as Formosa for the next four centuries.

The Dutch ruled Taiwan until 1661, when the Chinese pirate Cheng Cheng-kung and his army took control. Cheng Ching, Cheng's son, later took over. In the 1600s, many Chinese people came to Taiwan to escape wars and a lack of food in China. China's Ching **dynasty**, also known as the Manchus, sent troops to Taiwan in 1683. They fought Cheng Ching and took over Taiwan. In 1886, the Manchus declared that Taiwan was a **province** of China.

Above:
This picture shows Chinese pirates attacking a trade ship. Many pirates from China and Japan had bases on Taiwan because it was located along the main sea routes.

Japanese Rule

In 1895, the Chinese lost a war with Japan. They were forced to give Taiwan to the Japanese. In response, a group of Taiwanese people tried to turn Taiwan into an independent country. Soon, the Japanese army arrived, took over the capital city of Tainan, and ended the independence movement. The Japanese were harsh rulers, but they did improve Taiwanese industries, such as farming, and built new schools and roads.

Above: General Chiang Kai-shek (1888-1975) arrived in the Taiwanese city of Taipei on December 26, 1939. He was there for a meeting of China's ruling party, called the *Kuomintang* (KUO-min-dunk) Nationalist Party. At that meeting, Chiang was named head of China's government.

Taiwan After World War II

After World War II ended in 1945, Taiwan was given back to the Chinese. At first, the Taiwanese were happy to be free of Japanese rule, but they soon learned that China's Chiang Kai-shek and the Kuomintang were dishonest and cruel. In 1947, after many Taiwanese people **demonstrated**, secret Chinese forces killed as many as 28,000 people. **Communists** took over China in 1949. Chiang fled to Taiwan and took control. His harsh laws allowed few freedoms.

Below: Photographs on the walls of the Chiang Kai-shek Memorial Hall are a record of Taiwan's political history. The hall is located in Taipei, which is now the capital of Taiwan.

Modern Times

Until the 1970s, the United Nations (UN) still saw the Kuomintang as the official government of Taiwan and of China. The UN gave the Kuomintang's seat to China's communist government in 1971. By 1972, most countries saw Taiwan as part of communist China. In 1996, Lee Teng-hui won Taiwan's first direct presidential election. In 2000, Chen Shui-bian was elected president.

Below: Taiwan's new president, Chen Shui-bian (*left*), and his vice president, Annette Lu (*right*), celebrate winning Taiwan's second direct presidential election, which was held in March 2000.

Cheng Cheng-kung (1624–1662)

Cheng Cheng-kung brought Chinese laws and customs to Taiwan. He built Taiwan's first **Confucian** temple and also built many schools. During his rule, many people moved to Taiwan from the Chinese mainland.

Lee Teng-hui (1923–)

In 1988, Lee Teng-hui became ruler of Taiwan. In 1996, he became the first president elected by Taiwanese voters. He was also the first president who had been born in Taiwan. He lessened bad feelings between people who moved to Taiwan and the native Taiwanese.

Lee Teng-hui

Annette Hsiu-lien Lu (1944–)

After getting a law degree in Taiwan, Annette Lu studied in the United States. She later returned to Taiwan to run for election to the National Assembly. In 1979, she was put in jail for speaking out against the government. In 2000, Lu was elected vice president of Taiwan.

Annette Lu

Government and the Economy

Before 1996, the Kuomintang ruled Taiwan. Voters now elect a president, who heads all five *yuan* (YUEN), or branches, of Taiwan's government.

The Executive, Legislative, Control, Judicial, and Examination are the five yuans. The president picks a **premier** to lead the Executive Yuan. The premier and a council oversee the running of the government in general and decide on a set of rules for the government.

Above: Because Taiwan's economy is strong, many new buildings have been constructed, including the Taipei City Government Building.

Taiwan's Legislative Yuan makes the country's laws. The National Assembly also makes laws. It only meets to talk about large problems, however, such as removing a president from office. The Control Yuan oversees public services. It also investigates dishonest officials.

The Examination Yuan is in charge of the government's personnel system. It gives technology, civil service, and professional exams to people who want to work in the government. The Judicial Yuan heads the country's legal system. It oversees Taiwan's courts.

17

The Economy

Taiwan's economy is strong. Until the 1960s, most Taiwanese people worked in farming. As Taiwan began to sell more **exports**, many more industries started in the country. Between 1952 and 1999, Taiwan's economy grew faster than almost any other country. Most Taiwanese people now work in industries, including the **electronics**, clothing, and machinery industries.

Above: Chi-Lung Harbor is one of the largest seaports in the world. It was opened as a trade port in 1863.

Taiwan still produces some crops, including rice and tea. Fishing is also a large industry. Most products made in Taiwan, however, are electronics. The country produces electronics parts, such as **semiconductors**. It also makes whole electronic units, including digital cameras, computers, monitors, mice, and cell phones. Taiwan's technology is advanced. Millions of people in Taiwan use cell phones and the Internet.

Below: In 2000, 16 million people in Taiwan owned cell phones. The phones make it easy to keep in touch with family and friends.

People and Lifestyle

Most Taiwanese people are from the Chinese provinces of Fujian or Hakka. They came to Taiwan a long time ago. A smaller group of people came from China after World War II. To reduce bad feelings between the two groups, the people who came to Taiwan after the war are called "New Taiwanese." Only a small part of the population is made up of native Taiwanese people.

Below:
Many Taiwanese teenagers wear clothes like those worn in Western countries. Lots of people in Taiwan wear the current fashions and listen to the latest music.

Many native Taiwanese people have left their traditional jobs as hunters and farmers to work in factories. They often have modern clothes and habits as well.

In 2000, the population **density** of Taiwan was the second highest in the world, meaning that many people lived in a small area. Most Taiwanese people value patience and are respectful and friendly. Taiwanese people work very hard. In 2001, they worked an average of about 53.4 hours per week, about 11 hours more than the average American.

Family Life

Taiwanese families are usually small, with only one or two children. In the countryside, many family members often live in the same house, including children, parents, and grandparents. In the cities, many young people now have their own homes. In Taiwan, the father is the head of the household. His main job, however, is to be a good son to his own parents. The mother is in charge of raising the children. She sometimes gets help from the children's grandparents.

Above: Taiwanese families often take sightseeing trips around the country. Most families in Taiwan are small, with only one or two children.

Today, the role of women in Taiwan is changing. The cities offer women the chance to have jobs outside the home. Because of these jobs, many women are now able to support themselves. They have more choices and are more likely to end unhappy marriages.

Many Taiwanese families feel that getting divorced or letting others see family problems will make them "lose face," or be shamed, in the eyes of their community. Instead, they work hard to hide their problems from society.

Below: Elderly men gather in a park in Taipei. In Taiwan, older people are treated with respect by young people.

Education

Taiwanese children must attend school between ages six and fifteen. While in elementary school, they take subjects such as languages, arts, mathematics, nature, and technology. Beginning in fifth grade, students must take English. From first to sixth grade, they study a Taiwanese language. They can choose Fujianese or Hakka, which came from China, or a native Taiwanese language.

Below: Besides classroom learning, many Taiwanese children also join groups such as the Boy Scouts or Girl Guides, where they can pick up skills such as first aid.

When Taiwanese students complete junior high school at age fifteen, they may take an exam to enter senior high school, which is for students who plan to attend a university. The exam is also given for senior **vocational** school, in which students can study subjects such as art, music, farming, or nursing.

In Taiwan, students must compete to get into a university. They often attend extra classes and study hard to get high scores on college entrance exams.

Above:
Taiwan's oldest university, National Taiwan University, was built in Taipei in 1928. It was built by the Japanese.

Religion

Confucianism, Buddhism, and Taoism are the main religions in Taiwan. The practice of Confucianism is about 2,500 years old. It is based on the teachings of a man named Confucius. He taught lessons about morals, or the right ways to act. He believed that people should worship their **ancestors** and honor and respect heaven. Confucianism is often thought of as a set of rules to live by, instead of as an actual religion.

Above:
This religious man in traditional robes is asking for charity on a street in Taipei.

Buddhism was started in India by a man called Gautama Buddha, who taught people to **meditate** and to live simply. The religion came to Taiwan from China in the 1600s.

Taoism is a mix of Buddhism and traditional Chinese religions. During the time Japan ruled Taiwan, Taoists were not treated well. They began to worship secretly in Buddhist temples. By the time the Japanese left Taiwan, the two religions had blended together.

Below: A choir performs at a Christian church in Taipei. The Dutch and Spanish brought Christianity to Taiwan in the early 1600s.

Language

A great many people in Taiwan speak Southern Fujianese, which is a Chinese language. Taiwan's national language, however, is Mandarin. It is a language that came from Beijing, China. In each region of Taiwan, Mandarin is spoken slightly differently. Many native people in Taiwan speak Mandarin and a native language. Some native people no longer speak a native language at all. Taiwan's government has set up programs to help keep the native languages alive.

Above: Although many road signs in Taiwan are written in Mandarin and English, some of the signs do not make a lot of sense to English speakers.

Left: In parks and other public areas, notices are often put up on boards for older Taiwanese people to read. The notices are often the only way they can read about news and events.

Left: A woman is teaching her son how to write in the Mandarin language. Mandarin is written in columns from the top to the bottom of the page. It is read from the right-hand column to the left.

Literature

Shen Kuang-wen came to Taiwan in 1662. He brought traditional Chinese literature to the country and started a Taiwanese poets' society. During the Taiwanese New Literature movement of the 1920s, authors often wrote in several languages, including Japanese and Southern Fujianese. In the 1950s, during Chiang Kai-shek's rule, **lyrical** works and anticommunist literature became popular. Today, authors often write about the new, wealthy Taiwan.

Arts

Native groups in Taiwan create many kinds of art, including wood carvings, weavings, and baskets. The Paiwan and Rukai people are famous for their wood carvings, including snake designs that represent the rebirth of their ancestors. The Atayal people are famous for their weavings, which often have shell beads and metal bells in them. Old Chinese arts, such as dough sculpture and paper cutting, also are popular in Taiwan.

Below: Several of Taiwan's native groups are highly skilled in wood carving. This shop is selling statues of the Buddha, the man who started Buddhism.

Music and Dance

Native music in Taiwan is written about many parts of life, including love, daily work, and harvests. Native music often is played on drums, rattles, and stringed or flutelike instruments.

Taiwanese dances most often are held during ceremonies. Most dancers wear bright, colorful costumes, often with jingling bells on them. The dance steps usually are simple and include walking and foot stomping.

Above: In Taiwan, many children learn to play instruments at school. They may even join bands that perform at parades and other events.

Modern Arts

Before the 1960s, puppet shows were highly popular in Taiwan. Puppeteers traveled from town to town playing at events such as weddings, holidays, and temple festivals. Today, puppets are still an important Taiwanese art form.

Above: Performers in Taiwanese and Chinese operas often wear fancy costumes with colorful hats and heavy makeup.

Dragon dances are performed during celebrations, including the New Year festival. One dancer wears a dragon-head mask. Up to twenty-four dancers follow behind, wearing body sections covered in gold, green, or red fabric.

Taiwan is famous for Taiwanese and Chinese operas, which are performed at opera schools, community theaters, and temples. Taiwanese opera is only sung in Southern Fujianese. Chinese opera is performed in many forms of Chinese, depending on where it was written.

Opposite: Lion dance performers dress in colorful costumes and large, fancy masks. Many people believe the lion dance brings good luck. It is often performed at New Year festivals and public events, such as the opening of a new store.

Woodblock printing is a traditional art that has become very popular again. The prints are often of gods with mean-looking faces dressed in fancy clothing.

Leisure

Most Taiwanese people work hard, but they also like to have fun. Every year, many families go overseas. Taiwanese children also attend summer camps in other countries. To convince families to vacation in Taiwan, the government has built many sports and leisure centers.

Many Taiwanese people like to play computer games, use the Internet, and watch television. Walking, jogging, and practicing martial arts are also popular.

Below: Many people in Taiwan still enjoy the traditional sport of flying kites. Every year, thousands of kite lovers attend the colorful Taipei County International Kite Festival.

Left: Taiwanese people often enjoy going to the movies. Many people also enjoy listening to music, going on picnics, and hiking.

Traditional Games

Many games played in Taiwan are traditional Chinese games, including *diabolo* (di-a-BOH-loh). The diabolo looks like a small barbell and is rolled along a string tied between two sticks. It can be tossed into the air and caught.

Another Taiwanese game that came from China is **shuttlecock** kicking. The shuttlecock is most often kicked like a soccer ball, but some players do tricks with it. Many children also like to jump rope, spin tops, and play Chinese chess.

Below: *Taijiquan* (TY-chee-choo-en) is a traditional Chinese martial art practiced by many people in Taiwan.

35

Sports

Taiwanese schoolchildren must take physical education in school. They learn to play sports such as baseball, softball, volleyball, and martial arts. Popular martial arts in Taiwan include judo, tae kwon do, and kendo.

The Taiwanese are very good at a sport called dragon boat racing, which is now popular around the world. Other popular sports in Taiwan include scuba diving, surfing, and in-line skating.

Above: In Taiwan, big stadiums such as this one have been built to hold the thousands of fans who come to watch sporting events, including baseball games.

Baseball is also a very popular sport in Taiwan. It was brought to the country in the late 1800s. Today, many children join Little League teams at elementary and junior high schools.

Taiwan in the Olympics

At first, Taiwan could not compete in the Olympics because mainland China claimed Taiwan was also part of China. In 1958, mainland China pulled out of the Olympics. Taiwan then joined under the name "China." In 1984, Taiwan began using the name "Chinese Taipei."

Left: Yang Chuan-kwang (*right*) is probably the most famous Taiwanese athlete. He won a silver medal in the **decathlon** at the 1960 Olympics.

Festivals

Taiwanese festivals usually are held to honor events in history, gods, heroes, or dead ancestors. The Chinese New Year is the first major festival of each year. It lasts fifteen days, during which families like to gather. They also make offerings to gods. Chinese New Year ends with the Lantern Festival during the first full moon of the **lunar** calendar. Festivals honoring the Earth Gods and Medicine God are also held early each year.

Above: During the Chinese New Year, which is also called the Lunar New Year, shops sell many red paper decorations. The color red is supposed to bring good luck.

Left: These young men are holding up posters of Chiang Kai-shek while they march in a parade on Double Tenth National Day. The celebration is held on October 10, the day in 1911 when the Ching dynasty was taken out of power in China.

One of Taiwan's biggest festivals is the birthday of *Matsu* (MAH-tsoo), who is the goddess of the sea. Ceremonies are held in her honor at temples throughout the country. The Dragon Boat Festival attracts boat racing teams from around the world. During the Ghost Festival, it is believed that spirits visit the land of the living. Feasts and ceremonies are held for the spirits. In mid-fall, the Mid-Autumn Festival is celebrated. Families gather and often eat mooncakes, which are cakes shaped like the full moon.

Above: Festivals are often happy events in Taiwan. Street performers often wear bright, colorful masks and costumes and entertain the celebrators with songs and dances.

Food

Most food in Taiwan is served in bowls in the middle of the table. People then serve their food into their own bowls. Taiwanese meals are usually eaten with chopsticks and soup spoons.

Food in Taiwan is usually cooked in a Chinese style. Sichuan style and Hunan style Chinese food are popular in Taiwan. Sichuan style is usually hot and spicy. Hunan style can be hot and spicy or sweet and sour.

Below: In Taiwan, streetside food vendors are very common. Many of them make and sell desserts. After customers choose their ingredients, the shopkeepers often add shaved ice and syrup for a sweet treat.

Left: A restaurant sets out a display of stir-fried foods. Many restaurants in Taiwan set up displays of food in front of their shops to attract new customers.

Soups and seafood, pork, vegetable, and chicken dishes are very common in Taiwan. Many dishes are **stir-fried** and are flavored with ginger. Some dishes are made with garlic, hot peppers, and scallions, a kind of green onion. Most meals are served with rice. Tea is also commonly served with meals.

In Taiwan, favorite dishes include fried onion pancakes, rice with pork stewed in soy sauce, deep-fried bean curd, and deep-fried chicken parts.

Below: Many Taiwanese people believe that brewing and drinking tea is an art. They often use special tools, cups, and pots to make and drink the tea. Because tea is so popular, shops in Taipei sell many kinds of tea leaves.

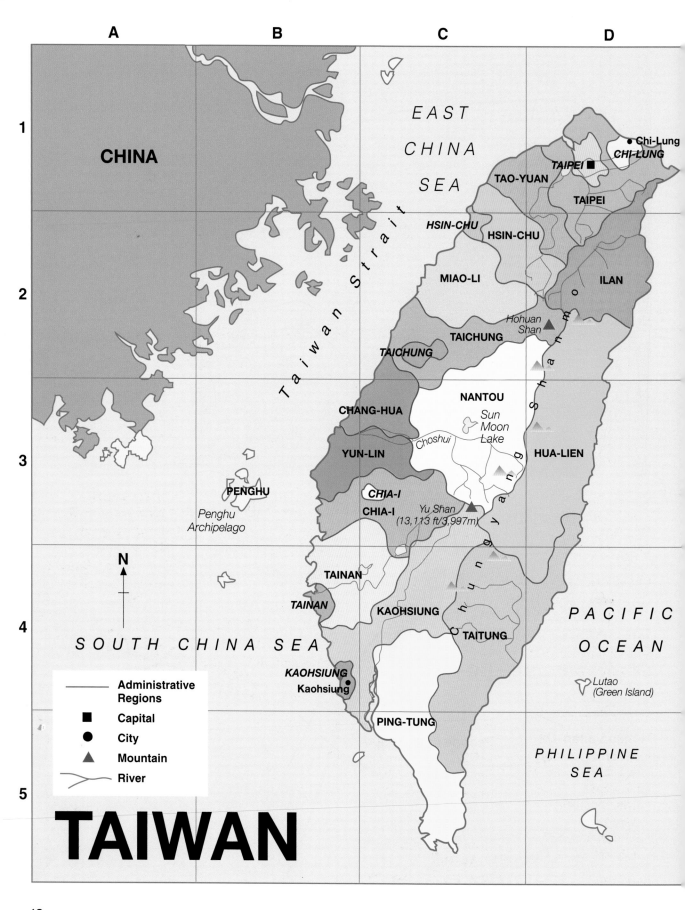

CHINA

EAST
CHINA
SEA

Chi-Lung
CHI-LUNG
TAIPEI
TAO-YUAN
TAIPEI

HSIN-CHU
HSIN-CHU

Taiwan Strait

MIAO-LI

ILAN

TAICHUNG
Hohuan
Shan
TAICHUNG

NANTOU
Sun
Moon
Lake
CHANG-HUA
Choshui
HUA-LIEN
YUN-LIN

PENGHU
CHIA-I
CHIA-I
Yu Shan
Penghu
(13,113 ft/3,997m)
Archipelago

N

TAINAN
TAINAN
KAOHSIUNG
TAITUNG
PACIFIC
OCEAN

SOUTH CHINA SEA
Lutao
(Green Island)
KAOHSIUNG
Kaohsiung

Administrative
Regions
Capital
City
Mountain
River

PING-TUNG

PHILIPPINE
SEA

TAIWAN

A   B   C   D

1

2

3

4

5

Above: Wen-Wu Temple is situated on the mountains beside Sun Moon Lake.

Chang-hua (county)
   B3–C3
Chia-i (county) B3–C4
Chia-i (municipality)
   C3
Chi-Lung D1
Chi-Lung
   (municipality) D1
China A1–C2
Choshui River B3–C3
Chungyang Shanmo
   C4–D2

East China Sea C1

Hohuan Shan D2
Hsin-chu (county)
   C1–D2
Hsin-chu
   (municipality)
   C1–C2
Hua-lien (county)
   C3–D4

Ilan (county) D1–D2

Kaohsiung (county)
   B4–C5
Kaohsiung (special
   municipality) B4

Lutao D4

Miao-li (county) C2

Nantou (county)
   C2–D3

Pacific Ocean D3–D5
Penghu (county) B3
Penghu Archipelago
   B3
Philippine Sea D5
Ping-tung (county)
   C4–C5

South China Sea
   A4–B5
Sun Moon Lake C3

Taichung (county)
   C3–D2
Taichung
   (municipality) C2
Tainan (county)
   B3–C4
Tainan
   (municipality) B4
Taipei (capital) D1
Taipei (county) D1–D2

Taipei (special
   municipality) D1
Taitung (county)
   C3–D4
Taiwan Strait B2–C2
Tao-yuan (county)
   C1-D2

Yu Shan C3
Yun-lin (county)
   B3–C3

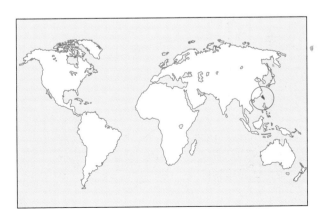

Quick Facts

Official Name Republic of China

Population 22,548,009 (2002)

Land Area 13,888 square miles (35,980 square km),
including Penghu Archipelago

Capital Taipei

Highest Point Yu Shan 13,113 feet (3,997 m)

Longest River Choshui

Official Language Mandarin Chinese

Major Religions Buddhism, Taoism, Confucianism

Administrative Regions Sixteen counties (Chang-hua, Chia-i, Hsin-chu, Hua-lien, Ilan, Kaohsiung, Miao-li, Nantou, Penghu, Ping-tung, Taichung, Tainan, Taipei, Taitung, Tao-yuan, Yun-lin), five municipalities (Chia-i, Chi-lung, Hsin-chu, Taichung, Tainan), two special municipalities (Kaohsiung, Taipei)

Famous Leaders Chiang Kai-shek, Lee Teng-hui, Chen Shui-bian

Festivals Chinese (Lunar) New Year, Double Tenth National Day, Dragon Boat Festival, Earth Gods Festival, Ghost Festival, Matsu's Birthday, Medicine God Festival, Mid-Autumn Festival

Currency New Taiwan Dollar (TWD $33.28 = U.S. $1 in 2004)

Opposite: This soldier stands guard at the Revolutionary Martyrs' Shrine in Taipei.

45

Glossary

ancestors: family members from the past, farther back than grandparents.

archipelago: a group of many islands.

communists: people who support a kind of government that owns and controls all goods and property.

Confucian: relating to Confucius and his teachings and followers.

decathlon: an athletic contest that has ten events, including several races and jumping contests.

demonstrated: joined in a group of people who were fighting against something they didn't like.

density: a measure of how tightly people or things are crowded into a space.

dynasty: a series of rulers who rule one after another over a long period of time and who are all from one family.

electronics: machines and equipment that run on electricity.

exports (n): products sent out of a country to be sold in another country.

lunar: relating to measuring months by watching the changes of the moon.

lyrical: relating to literature that could be set to music and sung as songs.

mainland: a continent or large piece of land, as opposed to an island.

martyrs: people who believed strongly enough in a religion or idea that they accepted death rather than give it up.

meditate: to sit quietly and think hard about a subject to gain knowledge.

monsoon: a strong, seasonal wind that sometimes brings heavy rains.

native: belonging to a land or region by having first grown or been born there.

premier: the highest official in the government, below the president.

province: a region of a country that is given fixed borders and its own local government officials.

semiconductors: materials that conduct electricity well at high temperatures but not at low temperatures.

shuttlecock: a light, cone-shaped object.

stir-fried: fried in a very hot pan while stirring constantly.

technology: using machines and science in everyday life, including doing a task using machinery.

vocational: related to an occupation, profession, or skilled trade.

More Books to Read

The Abacus Contest: Stories from Taiwan and China. World Stories series. Priscilla Wu (Fulcrum)

Buddha Stories. Demi (Henry Holt & Company)

Confucius: The Golden Rule. Russell Freedman (Arthur A. Levine)

Confucius: Great Chinese Philosopher. Anna Carew-Miller (Mason Crest)

Happy, Happy Chinese New Year! Demi Hitz (Crown Books)

Moonbeams, Dumplings, and Dragon Boats: A Treasury of Chinese Holiday Tales, Activities, and Recipes. Nina Simonds and Leslie Swartz (Gulliver)

Peanut Butter Friends in a Chop Suiey World. Deb Brammer (Bob Jones University Press)

The Prince Who Ran Away: The Story of Gautama Buddha. Anne Rockwell (Knopf Books)

Taiwan: Lisa Lin's Painting "Making Mooncakes." Young Artists of the World series. Jacquiline Touba (Rosen Publishing)

Taiwan in Pictures. Visual Geography series. Ling Yu (Lerner)

Videos

And the Gods Moved to Taiwan. Explore series (Valice Raffi)

Taiwan (Education 2000)

Taiwan (Questar)

Tug of War: The Story of Taiwan (WGBH)

Web Sites

deall.ohio-state.edu/bender.4/perform/ pg2puppe/bdx.htm

en.wikipedia.org/wiki/Taiwan

kidsdomain.com/holiday/chineseny.html

taiwandc.org/folk.htm

Due to the dynamic nature of the Internet, some web sites stay current longer than others. To find additional web sites, use a reliable search engine with one or more of the following keywords to help you locate information about Taiwan. Keywords: *Chiang Kai-shek, Kuomintang, Lungshan Temple, Penghu Archipelago, Taipei*

Index